GREAT DAYS IN THE ROCKIES

1　Self-portrait of Byron Harmon at a glacial lake in the Selkirks, n.d.

GREAT DAYS IN THE ROCKIES
The Photographs of Byron Harmon
1906-1934

EDITED BY CAROLE HARMON
AND THE PETER WHYTE FOUNDATION

WITH A BIOGRAPHY BY BART ROBINSON
AND AN APPRECIATION BY JON WHYTE

Toronto
OXFORD UNIVERSITY PRESS
1978

NOTE
In the title of this book, and occasionally elsewhere in the text, the term 'Rockies' is used collectively, for popular identification, to include not only the Rocky Mountains proper, but also the associated ranges of the Purcells and the Selkirks, which are separated from the Rocky Mountains proper by the Rocky Mountain Trench.

Canadian Cataloguing in Publication Data

Harmon, Byron, 1876-1934.
Great days in the Rockies

ISBN 0-19-540288-X

1. Harmon, Byron, 1876-1934. 2. Rocky Mountains,
Canadian — Description and travel — Views.*
3. Photography, Artistic. 4. Photographers —
Canada — Biography. I. Harmon, Carole, 1947-
II. Peter Whyte Foundation. III. Robinson, Bart.
IV. Title.

TR654.H37   779'.9'97110924   C78-001172-4

ISBN 0-19-540288-X
Printed in Canada by
T.H. BEST PRINTING COMPANY LIMITED

Preface

In 1974 I became concerned about the photographic collection of my grandfather, Byron Harmon, which consists of 6500 negatives on cellulose-nitrate base stock, an unstable and inflammable material. It was obvious that it needed immediate attention if portions of it were not to be lost. In 1975 I received the funding to preserve the collection. My work consisted of editing and preparing duplicates and contact prints of two-thirds of the negatives. I also selected and printed an exhibition of Byron Harmon photographs entitled 'In Mountain Light', which will be circulated by the Peter Whyte Gallery of Banff in 1978-80.

While I was in the final stages of my project, the Oxford University Press proposed publishing a book on Byron Harmon. It has been my great pleasure to work with the publisher and the Archives of the Canadian Rockies on the design and the selection of photographs for this book. For me the most exciting aspect of my grandfather's work is the sense that he was a storyteller who dramatized and recorded a tale of mountain life. I am delighted that the book reflects this.

I wish to thank those who provided the funding for the preservation of the Byron Harmon Collection: The Canada Council, Explorations; The Devonian Group of Charitable Foundations, Calgary; and Byron Harmon Photos, Banff.

I would also like to express my gratitude to all those people who, through their advice, encouragement, and enthusiasm, have helped in the execution of this project: Bob Alexander, The Banff Centre; Wilfred Bokman, The Canadian Conservation Institute; Edward Cavell; Barton Chapin; Ross Colquhoun; Bruce Ferguson, Dalhousie Art Gallery; Les Graff, Cultural Development Branch, Government of Alberta; E.J. Hart, Archives of the Canadian Rockies; Richard Huyda, Public Archives of Canada; Cathie Kobacher; José Orraca, University of Delaware; Bart Robinson; Alison Rossiter; Ryerson Polytechnic Institute; Chris Thomson; and Jon Whyte.

Finally, I owe my family special thanks for their loving support.

CAROLE HARMON

A Biographical Portrait of Byron Harmon

BART ROBINSON

When a twenty-seven-year-old itinerant photographer named Byron Harmon left a Canadian Pacific Railway coach at Banff, Northwest Territories, in 1903, he stepped into the right place at the right time.

He also stepped into a spot of extreme contrasts: a small, rough-hewn village, in the midst of a desolate mountain wilderness, which sported five first-class hotels and as bizarre an assortment of people as could be imagined. Pack-train outfitters in soiled chaps and beaten, wide-brimmed hats, stocky European alpinists in knickers and clunky nailed boots, and men and women of almost every nationality and race, all dressed in the latest fashions of their respective countries, intermingled in the short length of the dusty main street.

Banff, like the mountains that gave it birth, was midway between the era of earliest exploration and the age of mass commercialism. The David Thompsons and the Reverend Robert Rundles had come and gone, but the multitudes of highly mobile middle-class sightseers racing through the mountains at ever-increasing speed and in ever-increasing numbers had yet to arrive.

The Canadian Rockies in 1903 offered a playground for the not-so-idle rich and for climbers from England and Europe seeking first ascents comparable to those that had been exhausted in the Alps a decade earlier. They found new tracts of wilderness that had been charted and measured only in the most cursory manner by cartographers and scientists. Those who were

2 Self-portrait of Byron Harmon at Fortress Lake.
Columbia Icefield Expedition, 1924.

somehow afflicted found the promise of health in the mineral hot springs, which were guaranteed to be 'especially efficacious for the cure of rheumatic, gouty and allied conditions'. For a young photographer the Rockies offered a time and place of high excitement, wild-west romantic notions, and soaring mountains and shifting light to stir both spirit and eye. It was the beginning of a forty-year affair.

Byron Hill Harmon was born on February 9, 1876, near Tacoma, Washington, one of three children of Hill and Clara Smith Harmon. The parents were of pioneer stock, Clara's family journeying from Indiana to Washington in 1851 via the Oregon Trail, Hill's family following a more circuitous route to the West from New Brunswick and New York.

Clara exhibited all the characteristics expected of a child raised on a donation claim (let alone the second white person born on one of the islands of Puget Sound): resourcefulness and self-reliance, a respect for nature, and a compassion for others. She needed all of those qualities, for her husband disappeared shortly after Byron's birth and she was left with the sole responsibility for her three children. Working as a matron on one of the Puget Sound Indian Reservations, she kept her family together and exposed her children to the Indian character and native skills, an experience that would stand Byron in good stead in later years in the Rockies.

As a young boy Harmon had serious illnesses, suffering through typhoid on two occasions and struggling constantly against asthma. This affliction greatly influenced his decision to settle in the Rockies, where the clear, dry air granted him almost complete relief. The asthma stayed with him all his life, however, and occasionally when he returned to a coastal climate he suffered relapses so severe that he was forced to sleep sitting up in a chair to keep his lungs clear.

In his teens he exhibited two traits that would persist throughout his life: a predilection for working with his hands, creating and building objects of his own design, and a penchant for photography. Kodak marketed the first roll film in the late 1880s, and the company, using the slogan 'You Push the Button, We Do the Rest', went to great lengths to convince the American public that photography was no longer a science restricted to a professionally trained élite. Being unable to afford one of the advertised cameras, Harmon brought his talents to bear on a wooden box and fashioned a crude product of his own — a lensless pinhole affair that gave him his first images. Whatever the results of that early camera, they obviously encouraged him to continue with photography and, in fact, to turn to it for a living after a short stint working in a mill not only proved uncreative but also aggravated his asthma.

He opened a small portrait studio in Tacoma, probably in the mid-1890s, and the story of his humble beginnings as a professional photographer became a favourite one in his later, more comfortable years.

Once the young photographer had rented a building and equipped it with the necessary paraphernalia for developing and printing portraits, he was totally out of cash and well beyond his line of credit. Embarrassingly, he was a photographer without film for his cameras. Unperturbed, he welcomed his first client and calmly took a photograph *sans* film, receiving payment in advance. When the client returned the next day to collect the portrait, Harmon announced that he was not pleased with the results and that the process would have to be repeated. Another portrait was taken, this time with film purchased with the down payment, and Harmon was in business. Whether or not his ploy was a product of desperation or a premeditated risk or both, it exemplifies the ingenuity and confidence Harmon exhibited again and again in his photographic career.

Some time toward the end of the nineties, Harmon decided his asthma and his photography both needed a change of scenery. Reducing his studio to that which he could pack into two or three valises, he closed shop and left town — an itinerant photographer off to see the world. For two or three years he travelled thoughout the American Southwest and on to the eastern seaboard, to New York, and thence back west across Canada. His work was typical of the photography done in those days: stiff, formal Victorian portraits of couples and families, and slightly less formal poses of tradesmen standing, arms crossed, in front of the apparatus of their trade. It was not a lucrative way to make a living, but his presence would invariably arouse the collective curiosity of the small American and Canadian towns through which he travelled.

If Harmon's first visit to Banff was a short one, it was an important one. While soaking in the hot springs one day, he struck up a conversation with a local who informed him that despite the possibilities for a photographer in a town like Banff, there was as yet no permanent studio. Harmon was quick to recognize the potential for asthmatic relief in the high mountain air, and there is little doubt that the mountains themselves struck a highly responsive chord in him, for within a year he was back in what he termed 'that part of Canada which stands on end'. He embarked on his life's work: photographing every major peak and glacier in the Rocky and Selkirk Mountains in as many different moods and seasons as possible. It was a task that would end only when he could no longer travel deep into the mountain wilderness, over miles of limestone and quartzite ridges and peaks and across acres of tumbling, fissured glacial ice, the peculiarly turquoise-tinted lakes that might reflect twenty shades of light at any one moment, the fast-flowing silted rivers, and the deep glacier-scoured valleys.

Before returning to Banff to live, however, Harmon had some odds-and-ends to look after in the foothills, and he returned for a short while to High River, where he had been working before his mountain visit. There he exhibited a typical 'seize-the-

moment' impulsiveness by photographing a much-wanted gunman who had fled the U.S. and was creating no small concern in the towns along the eastern slopes of the Rockies. Hiding behind a stout brick chimney on a main-street roof, Harmon was able to photograph him undetected. The resulting print, of a wild-west desperado with a revolver on his hip, captured the imagination of the East and was carried by many of the major papers. It brought Harmon his first national recognition.

The combination of a healthy climate, magnificent scenery, and a chance to make a decent living must have had great appeal for Harmon. A long-time resident recalls the photographer as poor and in ill health when he returned to Banff. He was seen about town in a white shirt, overalls, a large straw 'sou'wester' hat, typical of those found in the American Southwest at the time, and short boots with no socks—a stocky man of medium height in peculiar clothes practising a peculiar trade.

Although he continued his portraiture in his first months in Banff, Harmon's photographic emphasis quickly shifted to the town's mountain setting and he began producing a line of 'mountain views' to sell to the tourists the Canadian Pacific brought to town. By 1907 he had accumulated enough views to advertise the largest collection of Canadian Rockies postcards in existence ('over 100 assorted views'), and he had saved enough money to pack away his valises and move into a tiny building on Banff Avenue that he converted into an effective working area by knocking a couple of skylights into the low shed roof.

From that time on, Harmon rarely took a formal indoor portrait. Only a few photographs of Stoney Indians, taken over the years at the annual Banff Indian Days, present full-frame, close-up visualizations of character; he was more interested in man in a larger context. Faces are frequently a part of his mountain photographs, but they almost inevitably appear as foils in an environmental drama. Harmon's preference was for landscape. 'I'd rather shoot mountains than people,' he would say, 'because mountains, at least, stand still.'

With his health much improved, he began to pursue the alpine pastimes of the day—hiking, riding, and climbing—but always carrying the heavy, awkward photographic equipment of the early 1900s: 4″ × 5″ and 5″ × 7″ view cameras (and, after 1910, a movie camera), wooden tripods, changing bag, extra film packs, and glass plates.

At the turn of the century Banff was a centre for mountain climbing, perhaps even more than it is today, because of the large number of unnamed and unclimbed peaks in the immediate vicinity. As a Victorian sport, climbing had no equal, and with all the great peaks of Europe conquered by the 1880s, alpinists turned their alpenstocks toward the unexplored regions of Canada. The CPR, not missing a trick, imported European climbing guides to escort tourists and alpinists to the summits of the Rockies and Selkirks, and such international figures as Edward Whymper of the Matterhorn became familiar faces in the Banff environs.

With so much activity in the area, it was only a matter of time before the sport became formally organized, and in March 1906 the Alpine Club of Canada was founded. After three years in the mountains, Harmon had become such an ardent alpinist and Rockies booster that he became a charter member of the Club and its official photographer, eager to use his skills to fulfil the dictates of the Club's charter, which called, among other things, for 'the cultivation of art in relation to mountain scenery' and 'the exploration and study of Canada's alpine tracts; and, with that in mind, ... [the gathering of] ... literary material and photographs for publication.'

The major event of the ACC's year was its climbing camp, held each year at a different spot in either the Rockies or Selkirks, featuring a week of exploring, hiking, and climbing. For most members it meant a moderately priced vacation in the mountains (all extended travel at that time was by pack train, an expensive proposition); for Harmon it meant a priceless opportunity to expand both his photographic and alpine experiences, and he rarely missed a summer camp during his early years of ACC involvement.

Harmon's work with the Alpine Club was critically important to his career because it opened up not only new territory for him but also important channels for recognition of his work. The *Canadian Alpine Journal*, distributed to members across North America and abroad, featured many of his photographs and, given the curiosity about the Rockies at the time, brought his images to the attention of alpinists, explorers, scientists, and editors throughout the world. And certainly the early ACC trips provided the basis for much of his collection, which today is made up of some 6,500 negatives and plates.

Club activities brought Harmon into close contact with the most colourful men in the Rockies, men who exerted great influence on his life: European guides such as Conrad Kain, Edward Feuz, and Rudolf Aemmer, men famous for their strength and daring who, collectively, never lost a single client; packers and outfitters like Jimmy Simpson, Bill Peyto, and the Brewster brothers, horsemen whose ability to turn an invective phrase against an 'ornery cayuse' never failed to astound the dudes and was matched only by their ability to bend the wilderness to meet their own ends; and explorers, scientists, and surveyors like Charles Walcott, secretary of the Smithsonian Institution, and A.O. Wheeler, founder, director, and first president of the Alpine Club and one of Canada's foremost surveyors and cartographers. From such men Harmon learned the secrets of mountain life, from the subtleties of the alpinists' knots and the packers' diamond hitch to the trick of drying wet matches in his hair. With them he formed his closest friendships—alliances that lasted long after his most active days on the trail.

His role as Club photographer gave Harmon a unique position

3   Setting up movie cameras to film an avalanche. Lake of the Hanging Glaciers Expedition, 1920.

in its hierarchy, and on several occasions he was asked to accompany special expeditions sponsored by the Club or its leaders. These trips had immeasurable importance for him, giving him a chance at extended travel in areas he probably wouldn't have seen by himself. Two journeys deserve particular mention.

In the fall of 1910, A.O. Wheeler asked Harmon to accompany a three-week trip into the Purcell Range, west of the Rockies and south of the Selkirks. The expedition had two purposes: to explore and map an area new to Wheeler, and to give a visiting Himalayan mountaineer and arctic explorer, Dr. T.G. Longstaff, a chance to hunt in the wilds of western Canada. In his memoirs, Longstaff remembers the mountains in 1910 as being at once beautiful and threatening:

> There is nothing more beautiful in any other mountain scene, but its menace is inescapable. The secret may lie in the density of the forests and their pathlessness: here is no reassurance of ancient tracks, no passes crossed by generations of caravans. The mountains of Europe and Asia recall gods and dryads and the long procession of man. These empty wilds are peopled only by our bare imagination, apt to primitive terror: there is no past except starvation.*

One man's menace, however, is another man's lure, and to all but the packers (who eventually had to turn back because they couldn't get the horses through the dense forests of the Purcells) the trip was an exciting and successful tour. Wheeler managed his survey; Longstaff was so successful in his hunting that modern conservationists cringe when reading how he took three grizzlies in one afternoon (an event that Harmon photographed and turned into a best-selling postcard); and Harmon got his photographs.

Just as the alpinists of the day were pleased to capture a new

peak by hand and rope, so Harmon was pleased to capture a new area on film, and the Purcells offered a particularly rewarding prize. Early in the trip, Harmon spent a day with the packers ahead of the main party clearing a trail for the horses. When he returned to camp that evening he was in an exultant mood. He had, he reported, discovered a massive glacier, the ice of which was pierced by what Longstaff later described as 'a collection of the most striking aiguilles I ever saw in the western mountains . . . [which] shot up from behind the glacier like arctic nunataks out of an icecap: quite sheer, without a speck of snow' (p. 231). The glacier, first known as Harmon's Glacier, is today called the Bugaboo Glacier and its expanse of ice and the surrounding peaks constitute one of North America's most famous climbing and skiing areas.

Descriptions of the trip written by both Longstaff and Conrad Kain, the party's alpine guide, provide the beginnings of a portrait of Harmon as a trail companion. Longstaff recalls him as 'a very good goer' and states that 'a hardier companion none could wish for'. Harmon was, as usual, 'inseparable from his beloved camera', and was indefatigable in his efforts to catch the images he wanted. A man of nearly boundless energy, he was more than willing to help the packers cut trail or to help rope up the horses 'as if they were tourists' and yard them up a particularly steep section of trail. On one occasion he hiked a continuous thirty-six mountain miles with full pack and camera gear, a feat few men would attempt, let alone complete!

He also possessed a keen, interested mind and a quirky sense of humour, traits that endeared him to those with whom he travelled. Though he is remembered as a quiet, private person, genial but slightly aloof, he was never above participating in the fireside activities so important to trail life. Both Harmon and Kain were mirthful souls at the fireside, and the two of them together had a special ability to keep a camp in high spirits. Kain, in *Where the Clouds Can Go* (published posthumously), remem-

---

*Tom Longstaff, *This My Voyage* (London: John Murray, 1950), p. 218.

bered the following scene after a particularly rough day on the Purcells trip:

> To improve our humour we held an Indian dance. Dr. Longstaff and the two packers put on bear hides and I the goat skin. Mr. Harmon, the photographer, was the band. His instrument the pans. So we danced about the fire, making a terrific din.*

The following summer Harmon again took to the trail with Wheeler and Kain in a larger party, including four scientists from the prestigious Smithsonian Institution, on a three-month trip to the Rainbow Mountains in what are now Jasper National Park and Mount Robson Provincial Park. The purpose of the expedition was threefold: Wheeler wanted to survey the region and investigate the Mount Robson environs as a possible site for a future ACC camp, and the Smithsonian men were interested in the flora, fauna, and geology of the area.†

It was a major trip into an uncharted region and, as might be expected, did not lack excitement. Kain described some of the problems in his diary, not the least of which was travelling with a photographer:

> Not incorrectly is this called the 'Wild West.' No houses, no roads; only old Indian trails. The valleys are wet and boggy, and one often sinks in to the knees. We have already ascended some mountains, *but the getting there!* On our first excursion we were almost buried by an avalanche, and Mr. Harmon had to photograph it at the very worst moment!‡

*Conrad Kain, *Where the Clouds Can Go*. Edited, with additional chapters, by J. Monroe Thorington (New York: The American Alpine Club, 1935), p. 273.

†It has been suggested that, once the fur trade was finished and the railway run through, there was only one reason for expeditions in the Rockies: to have a good time. The rest was rationale.

‡Ibid., p. 282.

This trip, Harmon's most extended mountain tour, was important, matched only by a trip to the Columbia Icefield thirteen years later. After ninety days in the wilderness even a mediocre photographer restricted to the valley bottoms could be expected to bring in a few decent plates. For an avid and seasoned photographer, on an expeditipn that scaled more than thirty peaks, there was bound to be an abundant harvest. And, judging from the results, Harmon was able to add credibility to his dictum that in order to know and photograph the mountains one had to walk through them, shooting them from the valleys up and from the summits down. Many of the finest prints in the collection date from this 1911 trip. Viewed collectively, they are a superb document of mountain travel and exploration. If one cares to look further, reading between the highlights and the shadows, one finds a special understanding of the mountains and what it means to measure one's life against them. The underlying exuberance of exploration, the dare and labour and ecstasy of the ascent, the challenge of the hunt, and the quiet days in camp are all there; but above all is the heady feeling of being *here*, in a vast and nameless place, close to the extreme leading edge of life. Harmon was not an articulate philospher, but these photographs of the broad rock faces and undulating glaciers, of men dwarfed on immense icefields, of climbers working on rock, snow, and ice, or weary but self-satisfied explorers resting in camp, speak eloquently for him.

Aside from the photographic aspects of the trip, two events occurred that were a source of great personal pride to Harmon. He and Kain achieved the first ascent of Mount Resplendent, at 3,362 metres a major peak in the Mount Robson area, and he was in the first party to cross through the mountains 'from steel to steel', from the Grand Trunk Pacific Railway at Fitzhugh (now Jasper) to the Canadian Pacific Railway at Laggan (now Lake Louise).

The ascent of Mount Resplendent was particularly gratifying, although the two men had to use a certain amount of dissimulation to make the climb. At the trip's outset, Wheeler had promised Harmon, Kain, and another well-know climber, the Reverend G.B. Kinney, a chance at the unclimbed Mount Robson, the highest peak in the Canadian Rockies (3,891 metres), if they would accompany the expedition. When the group reached the Robson area, however, Wheeler began to find excuses for keeping the men away from the big peaks. The trio became convinced that Wheeler wanted to save the major first ascents for a later ACC camp, and so it was that minor insurrections sprang up in camp. Harmon and Kain left camp one morning on the pretext of making a glacier reconnaisance in the great Robson amphitheatre and came back late with the ascent of Mount Resplendent secured. Kain added further fire to Wheeler's ill-suppressed fury when, a few days later, under the pretense of walking down the Emperor Falls gorge, he undertook a solo overnight climb of Mount Whitehorn, a climb he later described as 'one of the craziest and most foolhardy undertakings that I ever made in the mountains.'* Yet his rationale was easily understood by his alpinist companions: 'I could stand it no longer,' he wrote, 'being among beautiful mountains without climbing one.'

The return to Banff had its points of interest as well. Leaving Maligne Lake (now part of Jasper National Park) on September 18, a late start, the party encountered heavy snowfall in the high mountain passes close to the Continental Divide. Harmon found the logistics of moving a pack train through deep snow so photographically stimulating that years later, on his journey to the Columbia Icefield, he deliberately set out to duplicate the experience!

Trips such as the Purcell and Rainbow expeditions were exceptional opportunities and a far cry from the usual ACC climbing-camp endeavours, which Harmon enjoyed but ultimately found restrictive to his art. Travelling with large groups of people, keeping their pace (literally roped to their pace on the climbs), and going where they went often prevented him from catching the images he sought. His style required both a freedom to roam and a freedom to wait. An auspicious meeting of light and subject was not an event that occurred on demand, and on occasion Harmon's photographic 'lingerings' would become major feats of endurance.* Thus as years passed the photographer began to organize his own trips, making it clear to everyone at the outset that it was a photographic expedition to be taken at a photographer's pace. It should be noted, though, that Harmon remained a strong supporter of any group effort that would involve people with the mountains. He maintained close contacts with the ACC and was a founding member of both the Trail Riders of the Canadian Rockies, established in 1924, and the Sky Line Trail Hikers of the Canadian Rockies, organized in 1933.

Recognition came early. By 1908 the Banff paper, the *Crag and Canyon*, was keeping a close eye on the activities of the 'artistic photographer', and in 1910, Longstaff, in an article on the Purcells trip in the *Canadian Alpine Journal* (iii, 1911), opined that the expedition was 'fortunate in getting Mr. Byron Harmon ... whose Canadian mountain photographs are so deservedly popu-

---

Canadian Alpine Journal, vi, 1914.

*Walter Wilcox, in *The Canadian Rockies* (New York: G.P. Putnam's Sons, 1913), writes eloquently of the need for patience if one is to photograph the Rockies successfully: ' ... it is easy to prove that in an entire year there are only a few minutes, or at the most, a few hours in which the conditions are perfect for exposing a plate. Let us say that only during three months is the ground free of snow. Of these ninety days the large majority will be either stormy, or overcast, or very windy, and of the remainder some will be densely smoky, or too brilliant, so that the problem quickly narrows down to a possible ten perfect days. In each of these there will be only one or two hours in which the direction of sunlight is favourable for any given picture, and during these hours only a short time in which the ever-drifting clouds are properly grouped, the water surface unruffled, and the sunlight falling on foreground, or distance, or wherever you desire it to be' (p. 213).

4   Byron Harmon taking motion pictures in the Kananaskis Valley, n.d.

lar, to come with us....' His pictures of both trail life and activities in and around Banff were being picked up by the national news services and his widening circle of influential trail companions carried word of his work back home with them.

Harmon also gained stature through an impressive line of postcards,* viewbooks, and calenders that were mass produced by companies in Germany, England, and Vancouver at first, and later in his own Banff studio. Sales centred on the CPR, the only means of transportation through the Rockies in those days, and the railroad 'newsies' would peddle his works in the trains from Winnipeg to Vancouver. Catering to this market, Harmon produced viewbooks and cards collectively entitled 'Along the Line of the CPR', and included a railroad motif in many of the photographs.

In his personal and business life, Harmon maintained the same level of energy, ingenuity, and perseverance that he displayed on the trail. In 1908 he purchased an old livery barn across the street from his original location and converted it into a new and expanded darkroom and curio shop, and in 1912 he bought an adjoining lot on which he built a moving-picture theatre that featured not only 'fresh films daily', but variety nights and, during the Great War, various patriotic fund raisers. Unfortunately the theatre burned to the ground in January 1917. The fire cost Harmon an estimated thirteen thousand dollars and destroyed not only the theatre but portions of his working area next door, which meant a partial loss of his collection of stills and movie footage and most of his stock on hand. It was totally typical of the man, though, that within two or three days he had farmed out various phases of his business to different places in town and was back at work, plotting new schemes for his burned-out building.

Indeed, Harmon proved to be the archetyal free-enterprise entrepreneur. Seldom a year went by without some major renovation in the 'Harmon Block', and over the years his buildings included various combinations of the studio, a theatre, a curio shop, a drug store, a fountain lunch and tea shop, a book store and lending library, a woollen shop, and even a beauty parlour, many of them occupying a common area. His passion for designing and building fit in perfectly with the boom in technological gadgetry prior to the Great War, and he was forever trying out new ideas. His shops featured the first gas lights in Banff, the first ice-cream maker, the first neon sign, probably the first radio and phonograph, one of the first postcard machines in western Canada (capable of producing 4,000 cards a day), and God only knows what else. He designed and built much of the equipment used in his darkroom, built the screen used in the theatre, and devised an ingenious ventilating system for the theatre incorporating hollow beams that ran the length of the building. He was always amused to find that someone in town had 'borrowed' one of his business innovations for their own shop, and he would invariably smile and say, 'That's all right. There are plenty more ideas where that one came from.'

He was also somewhat of a speculator and at various times had amounts of money invested in drilling and mining operations. Receiving word that one such investment was not perhaps entirely above moral (and perhaps legal) reproach, he quickly pulled his shares and walked away with a good profit — in early 1929.

Making films was yet another vocation that Harmon pursued. Although nearly all of his footage has disappeared over the years, movies were important to him for both pleasure and profit. From the early teens on he devoted more and more time to film technique and technology, and some of his later journeys were

---

* The status of the postcard was considerably greater in the early 1900s than it is today. Between 1880 and the Great War the postcard had great appeal; and, in fact, a special word, 'delitilology', was coined to denote the study of postcards. Most of the early cards were printed in Germany, where the best lithography was done.

specifically referred to as movie trips. A fair portion of his footage was purchased by Fox Movietone News for national and international distribution.

Harmon's photographic ability and entrepreneurial inventiveness were matched by a strong sense of civic responsibility. Remembered by all as a 'model citizen', he was a founding member of the Banff Board of Trade (a forerunner of both the Chamber of Commerce and the Banff Advisory Council), a member of the school board for many years, an organizer of the Banff Conservative Association, a charter member of the Rotary Club, a major investor in a newspaper meant to compete with the *Crag and Canyon* (making him an unwilling participant in an ensuing political feud), and a member of numerous other local committees, boards, and associations. For its part, the town was more than pleased with its photographer, who was keeping Banff well in the eye of the North American press. As the *Crag* put it in 1919:

> Bryon Harmon is the best asset Banff has in the line of advertising the village to the outside world. Nothing of importance occurs but he is present with his movie camera, and the Harmon films of Banff and the mountains are becoming known wherever there is a movie house.

In the same year he received the culminating recognition of his career. The Government of Canada, with the Alpine Club of Canada, asked Harmon to be one of four representatives to the International Congress of Alpinism in Monaco in May 1920. The trip was a triumph. His old trail companion, Wheeler, reported in the *Canadian Alpine Journal* (xi, 1920):

> With the whole-hearted assistance of Mr. Harmon your director was enabled to arrange a magnificent exhibit of photographic enlargements, some 150 in number, of the most striking scenic features of the Canadian Rocky Mountains,

comprised chiefly of Mr. Harmon's beautiful pictures and unsurpassed motion films. . . .

The exhibition was, by all reviews, a show-stopper, particularly the movies. According to Wheeler, 'they carried his audience off its feet and [Harmon] was called on to show them again and again throughout the duration of the Congress.'

Monaco, as it turned out, was but one of several locations in which the exhibit received rave reviews. On his way there Harmon had exhibited his prints on the floor of the Canadian House of Commons (selling prints to nearly all the members of Parliament), and after the Congress he showed his films before the Royal Geographical Society in London and the Royal Scottish Geographical Society in Glasgow, Aberdeen, and Edinburgh.

On the strength of the 1920 jaunt, Harmon returned to Europe in the winter of 1923-4, exhibiting prints and showing films in the major centres of France, Germany, and Great Britain and returning with contracts for over 15,000 feet of film — no small amount in the early twenties. The mountain photographer had arrived.

Despite his successes, Harmon remained a quiet and modest person, the sort of man, according to old-timers, whom one might take for granted. An immaculate dresser in town, a near teetotaller and non-smoker, he avoided the social activities of Banff, preferring to spend his time with his family* or his work. Not that he was unfriendly; he merely had other things on his mind than curling, cards, and dancing, the three major Banff social pastimes.

One of the things on his mind, of course, was his continuing work with the Rockies and the Selkirks. Harmon told Lewis

---

* His first marriage was to Maud Moore in either 1909 or 1910. Three children—Aileen, Lloyd, and Don—were born in 1912, 1914, and 1917. Don was born on the same night the theatre burned down, something Harmon used to tease him about: 'Worst time of my life,' he would say, 'two disasters in one night.' A second marriage, to Rebecca Pearl Shearer, took place in Seattle in 1928.

Freeman, a freelance writer and adventurer, of his master plan in the late summer of 1920 when the two men met at the Lake of the Hanging Glaciers. He had allotted himself twenty years to photograph every major peak and glacier in the Rockies and Selkirks and, having finished the first run-through, would be ready to start all over again. At their first meeting Harmon was sitting out a seemingly interminable period of bad weather — waiting, as he so often did, for the light. Freeman took note of the wait and later wrote:

> It was in that quiet, patient, persistent way that he had been photographing the mountains of the Canadian West for many years, and it will be just in that way he will continue until he shall have attained somewhere near to the high goal he has set for his lifework....It is a privilege to have met an artist who works with so fine a spirit, who has set himself so high an ideal.*

Whereas the early exploring sessions with Wheeler had been exciting, Harmon's later photographic and movie trips were adventurous to the point of danger. He was forever ready to set up a shot to capture the most romantic implication of any given event. If there existed a choice between doing something an easy way or doing it in an arduous but more visually exciting way, Harmon would invariably opt for excitement.

Nor was he against accelerating the course of nature occasionally to suit his purposes. In 1922 he joined forces with his old friend Conrad Kain and two clients from Minneapolis on a pack-train trip to the Lake of the Hanging Glaciers to film a massive avalanche. He had confidence that just such an occurrence might happen while he was at the lake, since he and Kain had secreted thirty-six sticks of dynamite into the pack duffel. Cora Best, one of the Minneapolis dudes, graphically described

* Lewis Freeman, *On the Roof of the Rockies* (New York: Dodd, Mead and Co. 1925), p. 11.

the resulting high comedy for the *Canadian Alpine Journal* (xiii, 1923):

> Conrad went over and dug a hole in the ice and placed his dynamite, tamped it down and lighted the fuse. When he came back he remarked that something should come loose as there were seventeen sticks about to let go. Harmon took a last anxious look into the finder....He mopped his face and looked along the line to see if everything was ready. It was....The earth shook, the air turned purple: Mother Nature agonized, and a few pounds of ice tinkled off into the water as the smoke drifted away. But, of course, that was understood. We were waiting for the aftermath, the mighty avalanche we were sure to get.
>
> Now, when Old Bill [a pack horse] had been unloaded he had strolled off to browse on some tufts of green and no one had given him a second thought. When the first report of the discharge took place, Old Bill started a little charge of his own....He came down the stretch hitting on all fours, his mane flying, his nostrils dilated and flaming, his eyes holding the fire of battle. He hit Harmon first! Down went the camera and Old Bill walked up the spine of the vanquished photographer, hit the second, third and fourth cameras with sickening precision and careered off down the valley. And then it happened! The whole top of the mountain eased off a bit, toppled and crashed to the glacier below in the mightiest of mighty avalanches.

Harmon organized his last extended trip into the mountains in 1924 — a seventy-day 500-mile trip to Jasper via the Columbia Icefield and the headwaters of the Athabasca River — hoping to photograph the last remaining obstacles to the completion of his work: the mountains and glaciers of the Columbia Group. With two or three major deviations, the route followed the line of the Icefields Parkway that runs today from Lake Louise to Jasper.

Of all his trips, it is the best documented, for accompanying Harmon was Lewis Freeman, who wrote an unfortunately exaggerated account of the expedition for the *National Geographic* (using many of Harmon's photographs) and later wrote *On the Roof of the Rockies*, about the trials and tribulations of the trip. The book is dedicated 'To Byron Harmon, who, through his photographs, has given the Canadian Rockies to the World'.

Harmon's propensity for the exciting shot led them into some rather peculiar situations. Forgoing the obvious and easy river fords, Harmon would repeatedly ask the packers to drive the horses through some slightly rougher waters, in one case driving a good portion of the pack train into, around, and under a log jam. On another occasion, failing to get the desired footage of a mountain goat's being shot and falling off a high precipice, Harmon had his companions rig up a goat carcass so it would 'leap' off a cliff while being filmed from below. The goat leapt, all right, and came within millimetres of driving Byron a good distance into the glacial ice he was shooting from.

The pack train was also outfitted with a radio and passenger pigeons,* Freeman wishing to prove that radio reception was possible in the wilds of the western mountains, and Harmon wanting to see if the pigeons could thread their way through the peaks back to Banff. The radio worked extremely well, both as a receiving instrument and as a prop for an endless array of photographs, but the pigeons were a major disappointment.

One other experiment consisted of crossing a glacier tongue with the pack horses. This improbable action was taken both to give the party a better look at the mother icefield, the Colum-

bia, and to avoid travelling an alternate route consisting of forty miles of flooded river flats. Although some problems were encountered in getting the horses off the glacier, where they had to slide down a narrow ramp of ice flanked by deep crevasses, the traverse went smoothly and Harmon put the event to good photographic use.

Despite the adventures, or misadventures, of the journey, the expedition was successful, right down to the calculated snow storm in Jonas Pass on the way home, and Harmon returned with 400 stills and some 7,000 feet of film. It was somehow fitting that he had been forced to wait eight days for the light to reach Mount Columbia, the second highest peak in the Rockies, the monarch of the Icefield, and one of the last mountains he felt he needed in his collection. It wasn't until the afternoon of the eighth day, after time, food, and patience were exhausted and the pack train had been sent on down the valley, that Harmon, lingering behind, caught his image. The light played on the summit for less than forty minutes. At the end of those few minutes, Freeman recalled, 'The black rectangles of paper torn from Harmon's film-packs were piled up behind his tripods like the brass shells around a hard-pumped machine gun at the end of a battle.'

Harmon did not abandon the mountains after his 1924 Icefield trip. Winter and summer he was out with dog team and pack horse, with skier and hiker, but the Icefield expedition was his last extensive exploratory journey. He found that his business required more and more time, as did his desire to see new places and experience new things. Nearly every year from the mid-twenties on he managed a major trip outside the mountains, often travelling to the American Southwest, but often as not to more remote, exotic spots: Mexico, Guatemala, Hong Kong, Europe, and once, in 1930, around the world. No matter where he went, he always insisted upon his return that the Rockies were the best of all and, indeed, wherever he went he carried

*Harmon was an avid naturalist and was sympathetic to all forms of animal life — so much so, in fact, that he never owned a rifle and would hunt only when absolutely necessary. Throughout his life he kept various pets, including dogs, pigeons, and a squirrel that used to ride in his coat pocket. At one point he brought home a porcupine for his children, and deer were always encouraged to wander into his house from the street to eat food scraps in the pantry.

photographs and films to show all who might be interested.*

His last years in Banff were relatively quiet ones. High blood pressure and diminishing sight and hearing troubled him increasingly, but he remained a keen and interested observer of things around him. His love of the mountains and its inhabitants burned as brightly as ever, as did his own particular sense of humour. His son Don one day reproached him for swatting at flies that were on the outside of a screen door and Harmon retorted, smiling, 'Well, this way, you see, I stun their legs. Then they fall to the sidewalk and break their necks.'

During the spring of 1942 his health took a turn for the worse and he was admitted to the hospital several times for high blood pressure. It was not easy for a man with such vitality and so much interest in life to accept the inevitable slowing down, and he lamented to a visiting friend one day that there seemed to be no compensation for good living.

His death on July 10, 1942, at the age of sixty-six, was sadly noted by his old acquaintance A.O. Wheeler in the *Canadian Alpine Journal* (xxviii, 1943): 'In the art and science of photography,' he wrote, 'he was outstanding *par excellence*....We liked him well and shall not readily forget him and the living record of his life work.'

*A promoter to the end, Byron once left for the Southwest with his car 'specially arranged for the tour with the best and latest view of Lake Louise filling the right hand window . . . a panoramic view of the Bow River filling the back window, and a picture of Mount Columbia in the left window....' (*Crag and Canyon*, 1938).

5 Byron Harmon waiting for the light at Amethist Lake, 1918.

I   With the Alpine Club of Canada

Harmon had been living in the mountains a little less than three years when, in March 1906, the Alpine Club of Canada put out a call for charter members. Signing on as one of seventy-nine original subscribers, he became the Club's official photographer, an act that proved to be a critically important step in his career.

The Club's charter set forth five major goals: (1) the scientific study and exploration of Canada's alpine and glacial regions; (2) the cultivation of art in relation to mountain scenery; (3) the education of Canadians to an appreciation of their mountain heritage; (4) the encouragement of the mountain craft and the opening of new regions as a national playground; and (5) the preservation of the natural beauties of the mountain places. To promote its objectives the Club held annual climbing camps, and each summer the alpine faithful would troop off to a different spot in the Rockies or Selkirks to enjoy a week of hiking, climbing, and exploring in what were then relatively untouched areas. The Club also sponsored major scientific and exploratory expeditions and published an annual report, the *Canadian Alpine Journal.*

The organization constituted an ideal set-up for a budding landscape photographer without much money, and Harmon was an eager participant in both the early climbing camps and the more extended scientific trips. To a large extent the Club served as Harmon's patron at a time when he needed one badly, affording him a chance to travel to and photograph areas he wouldn't have seen by himself. It also brought him into close contact with the great personalities of the Rockies, from whom he learned his mountain skills and with whom he formed his closest friendships.

The longer scientific and exploratory journeys were of particular consequence for Harmon, and the photographs of the three-week trip to the Purcells in 1910 and the three-month expedition to the Rainbow Mountains in 1911 form an important part of the existing Harmon collection.

With the passage of years, Harmon found the Club's climbing-camp format restrictive to his style, and his involvement with the group diminished considerably after 1918, when a Photographic Committee was formed. He retained his close contacts with the Club and its leaders, however, and attended the summer camps whenever his schedule would allow.

6 Climbers on the summit horn of Mount Resplendent.
Mount Robson ACC Camp, 1913.

7 Alpine Club members near the Giant Steps. Paradise Valley ACC Camp, 1907.

8 Climbers traversing a snow slope of Mount Huber.
Lake O'Hara ACC Camp, 1909.

9 Studying a map in camp.
'Longstaff — Wheeler' Bugaboo Expedition, 1910.

10 (*right*) Around a smudge at Calumet Creek.
ACC — Smithsonian Robson Expedition, 1911.

11   Marmolata, Pigeon and Snowpatch Spires and the Bugaboo (Harmon) Glacier.
'Longstaff – Wheeler' Bugaboo Expedition, 1910.

12   Ridge of Mount Resplendent, c. 1911.

13 Two men in a crevasse on the Bow Glacier.
ACC Bow Valley and Yoho Expedition, 1910.

14 Climbers looking into a crevasse on the Robson Glacier.
Mount Robson ACC Camp, 1913.

15   Two men looking up at a hanging glacier. Yoho Valley ACC Camp, 1910.

16 Climbers silhouetted against the Yoho Glacier. Upper Yoho ACC Camp, 1914.

17   Climbers on Mount Huber. Lake O'Hara ACC Camp, 1909.

18 Alpine Club members looking at Emperor Falls.
Mount Robson ACC Camp, 1913.

19 Climber looking down the Robson Glacier.
Mount Robson ACC Camp, 1913.

20 Climbers below an icefall on Mount Robson.
Mount Robson ACC Camp, 1913.

21 East face of Mount Robson.
ACC – Smithsonian Robson Expedition, 1911.

22 Conrad Kain, Albert H. MacCarthy and William W. Foster after the first
ascent of Mount Robson. Mount Robson ACC Camp, 1913.

II Along the Line of the CPR

The development of the Canadian Rockies as a scenic playground and the coming of the Canadian Pacific Railway to the mountains were closely related: the one grew out of the other. As soon as the last spike was driven at Craigellachie in 1885, the CPR was faced with the problem of enticing people to ride the new line, and it was to the western mountains the company looked for a solution.

By virtue of a massive promotion campaign and the construction of a series of Swiss-style chalets across the Rockies and Interior Ranges, the CPR was most effective in creating a vacation mecca where only a few years before there had been nothing but untrodden wildlands. Banff, with its mineral hot springs, was a prime spot for development, and the railway pushed for the creation of a national park around the village in 1887. Within a very few years people from all corners of the world were flocking to the area to soak in the mineral springs and 'recreate' in the midst of 'The Canadian Pacific Rockies'.

The CPR was generous with its customers. Not only were the service and appointments in both the trains and the hotels as fine as could be found in the world, but the company was forever adding new and ingenious touches to an already lavish system. Company crews cut riding and hiking trails through the mountains and built a number of tea-houses in which weary travellers could rest and refresh themselves, and the company imported European mountain guides to take visitors to the summits of the mountains they had journeyed so far to see.

The railroad constituted the life blood of Banff for the first three decades of the century and it was only natural that the town should cater to the railroad clientele. Harmon used the CPR as a focal point for much of his early business, and many of his first view books and postcards bore the title 'Along the Line of the CPR', and featured railroad-related activities in the mountains. The books and cards were distributed on the trains from Winnipeg to Vancouver and were an important source of income for Harmon in the early years.

One interesting series of photographs that was *not* peddled by the CPR dealt with a 1910 avalanche in Roger's Pass. Company track crews were attempting to clear the tracks of the debris brought down by one avalanche when another larger slide came down and buried the men. Harmon recorded the rescue attempt, achieving some interesting, if untypical, material.

23   Train ascending the Kicking Horse Canyon, n.d.

24 Lake Agnes Tea-house, n.d.

25 Banff Springs Hotel, c. 1920.

26   Tally-ho at the Banff Springs Hotel, c. 1910.

27   (*right*) Bathers at the Cave and Basin, Banff, c. 1910.

28 'Rocky Mountain Tours and Transport' sightseeing cars on the Vermilion Lakes Road near Banff, 1924.

29 Mount Rundle and Echo Creek, n.d.

30   Horse race at Banff Indian Days, c. 1920.

31 American Shriners on a locomotive at Banff Station, 1923.

32 Three men shovelling snow off the roof of Glacier House at Glacier, B.C., 1925.

33 Man beside 'snow mushroom' near Glacier, B.C., 1925.

34   (*left*) Workmen clearing an avalanche on the
railroad line near Rogers Pass, 1910.

35   Snowplough and workmen clearing the same
avalanche as opposite, 1910.

36 Lake Louise Chalet with the Victoria Glacier beyond, c. 1920.

37   Elsie Brooks with a bear, c. 1920.

III   Mountain People

Byron Harmon's people are comfortable in their setting: subjects who have not been asked to mask themselves in their anticipations of what the world thinks of them or wants them to be.

The Indians in this section are Stoneys, a tribe of Assiniboines who live in the eastern foothills of the Rockies. Most of the pictures were taken during Banff Indian Days, an annual event during which members of various tribes come to Banff for three or four days of parades, rodeo events, dances, games, and to be photographed. The man in makeup with the Sundance paraphernalia arrayed before him is one of the only two existing photographs from a longer series Harmon took of the religious celebration. The rest have unfortunately disappeared.

The whites in Harmon's photographs are a mixture of all the sorts of people the mountain West attracted: wranglers, guides, and outfitters who eked out a life by providing services to the visitors; the Swiss Guides whom the CPR hired to 'alpinize' the Rockies and Selkirks; and some of the visitors themselves: Alpine Club members, adventurers, explorers, hunters, railwaymen, fishermen. Phimister Proctor, an American painter and sculptor, was incidentally in the Maligne Lake area at the same time as Harmon. In Canada to study the buffalo at Wainwright, he is not typical of the artists the CPR imported to the Rockies to record the mountain playground.

In Harmon's portraiture there is neither the arrogance of pomp nor the artifice of inhibition. There is, as a consequence, little loss of dignity. Only in 'Mrs. Griffith' (Plate 46) do we detect any aspect of irony, and we suspect she would never have seen it.

38   Hunters with dogs on a summit near Jumbo Creek, n.d.

39 Preparing for a Sundance, n.d.

40 Stoney Indians at Banff Indian Days, n.d.

41   Mrs Job Beaver and child, 1934.

42   Isaac Rollinmud, n.d.

43 John Salter, c. 1925.

44 Young Stoney Indians, n.d.

45   Widow Chiniquay at Banff Indian Days, n.d.

46 Mrs Griffith at Yoho ACC Camp, 1906.

47 Christian Hasler Jr (*left*) and Ernest Feuz (*right*) with unidentified client above the Fox Glacier, n.d.

48 Fishermen in the Kananaskis Valley, n.d.

49 Phimister Proctor painting on the shore of Maligne Lake.
ACC – Smithsonian Robson Expedition, 1911.

50 George Harrison standing under a promontory
above the Illecillewaet Valley, c. 1920.

IV   The Wilderness

A still untrammeled, scarcely explored, barely exploited world awaited Byron Harmon when he reached Banff and the Rockies. The early years were over. By the time he finished his work in the 1930s the number of visitors to the mountains had increased many times.

The physical world he photographed has remained much the same. An occasional glacial recession may be visible, but the social and human world he entered was evanescent. Harmon's records of the pack trips, climbing expeditions, and hunting parties would not be so important had the entire texture of wilderness travel not altered so much in the years since his expeditions.

The wildlands had an overwhelming appeal for Harmon because of the richness of scenery they presented and the types of activities which occurred within them. A land of changing effects, surprise around each corner of the trail, laden with possibilities for photographing the unusual, the wilderness became a wonderful surface to play on.

His photographs combine at their best two elements: people involved in a mountain-oriented activity such as snowshoeing, climbing, hunting, or just wandering, and the grandeur of the setting in which those activities took place. He staged his photographs, of course, setting up the right activity in the proper landscape, waiting for the proper atmosphere; but never so artificially that we feel the photograph is false.

51   Mount Quincy. Columbia Icefield Expedition, 1924.

52   Man on an ice overhang at the mouth of an ice cave
in the Starbird (Horsethief) Glacier.
Lake of the Hanging Glaciers Expedition, 1920.

53   Teepee at Maligne Lake. Columbia Icefield Expedition, 1924.

54   Teepee at Mount Assiniboine, n.d.

55 A.O. Wheeler and T.G. Longstaff with three dead grizzly bears.
'Longstaff – Wheeler' Bugaboo Expedition, 1910.

56 T.G. Longstaff, Bert Barrow, and Charles Lawrence scraping grizzly-bear hides. 'Longstaff – Wheeler' Bugaboo Expedition, 1910.

57 Man with dog on top of an icewall at the Lake of the
Hanging Glaciers. Lake of the Hanging Glaciers Expedition, 1920.

58   Jimmy Simpson, with Scotty Wright, skinning a goat near Ptarmigan Pass, 1920.

59   Jimmy Simpson, with two unidentified men,
skinning a goat near Howse Peak, 1917.

60   Ike Mills and his dog team with a skier near Mount Assiniboine, 1934.

61   (right) Ike Mills and his dog team on Ptarmigan Lake, 1932.

62 Two men in an ice-cave, n.d.

63 Three climbers on seracs of the Illecillewaet Glacier, n.d.

64 Mount Hungabee, n.d.

65 Christian Hasler Jr, unidentified boy and
Ernest Feuz climbing Mount McGill, n.d.

66 Truck carrying a canoe at Sinclair Canyon on the
Banff-Windermere Highway. Kootenay River Expedition, 1923.

67   Two men canoeing and one man fishing from the shore
on the Cross River. Kootenay River Expedition, 1923.

68 Man snowshoeing on the Johnston Canyon trail
near Pilot Mountain, 1930.

69   The Goodsir Towers, Mount Goodsir, 1923.

V The Columbia Icefield Expedition, 1924

High astride the Continental Divide, approximately halfway between Lake Louise and Jasper, lies the Columbia Icefield, a massive sea of ice covering an area of nearly 110 square miles, making it the largest icefield in the Canadian Rockies. The Icefield and the surrounding summits of the Columbia Icefield Group constitute for many people the scenic culmination of the mountains. Harmon referred to it as 'one of the most awesome and picturesque regions in the world'.

Discovered in 1898 by the British alpinist J. Norman Collie, the Icefield remained for many years a remote, mysterious, and almost inaccessible spot; even as late as the early twenties only a handful of men had trod its glacial waste. For Harmon, intent on capturing on film the major peaks and glaciers of the Rockies and Selkirks, the Icefield environs were a must. During the autumn of 1923 he organized a major pack-train trip for the following summer, planning to journey from Lake Louise to Jasper and back, with a month-long stopover at the Icefield. Also on the itinerary was the crossing of a glacial tongue with the pack train, a visit to the headwaters of the Athabasca River and Mount Columbia, the second elevation in the Rockies, and a late 'snowscaped' return to Banff.

This trip, Harmon's last extended mountain tour, was both exciting and productive, and the photographer returned with 400 stills and 7,000 feet of movie footage after seventy days and 500 miles on the trail. Of all his mountain travels, the Icefield journey remained Harmon's most memorable trip.

70   Ulysse LaCasse looking at a waterfall on the Castleguard River.
Columbia Icefield Expedition, 1924.

71 Crowfoot Glacier with packtrain in foreground. Columbia Icefield Expedition, 1924?

72   Teepee at Bow Lake, Columbia Icefield Expedition, 1924.

73   Fording a river. Columbia Icefield Expedition, 1924.

74   (*right*) Packtrain on a moraine near the Saskatchewan Glacier. Columbia Icefield Expedition, 1924.

75 Horses in 'smudge'. Columbia Icefield Expedition, 1924?

76 Mount Columbia and the headwaters of the Athabasca River.
Columbia Icefield Expedition, 1924.

77 Soapy Smith, Lewis Freeman, Ulysse LaCasse and Bob Baptie at the toe of the Saskatchewan Glacier. Columbia Icefield Expedition, 1924.

78   Packtrain crossing the Saskatchewan Glacier. Columbia Icefield Expedition, 1924.

79 Ulysse LaCasse with packhorses floundering in heavy snow near Poboktan Creek. Columbia Icefield Expedition, 1924.

80 (*right*) Packtrain climbing Jonas Pass. Columbia Icefield Expedition, 1924.

81   Mount Bryce and the Columbia Icefield, from Mount Castleguard.
Columbia Icefield Expedition, 1924.

An Appreciation

JON WHYTE

The Harmony Drugstore in Banff still exhibits the wooden-framed enlargements of Byron Harmon's photographs which were my introduction to the mountain world beyond the narrow Bow Valley. Those photographs, many of which are reproduced in this book, contained mysteries of dog sleds, pack trains, hunters, explorers, and climbers; they were the openings to romance, a world both threatening and inviting. We built stories around them then. About the image of the climbers on Mount Resplendent (Plate 12), for example, we thought: 'Because the clouds were all around them, they kept on climbing even after the ridge was gone. When the clouds went up again, there was no sign of them.' (Were we remembering Odell's last sighting of Mallory and Irvine disappearing into the clouds near the summit of Everest in 1924? It was a familiar story in our household. And it may be what misled us into believing the climbers were *ascending*.) I can look at the same photograph now and analyse the composition of lines which invariably draws our eyes up and into the vanishing point in the peak-concealing clouds, but the temptation to read a fiction in the image persists.

Harmon was a storyteller, but he placed the story foremost, telling it with such a sense of inevitability we forget a narrator is behind the mask of stylelessness. Certainly the photographs are rich in style; but rather than imposing the style, Harmon derives it from the particularities of scene, actors, or action. Looking at the photographs, we are comfortable in works where a sense of form enhances subject or scene, where perception of textures and the play of light upon them make the lack of colour irrelevant.

If Harmon's photographs have an easy familiarity, it's probably because for years the standard views of the Rockies and Selkirks were his, broadcast to the world by postcard, viewbook, and hand-tinted framing prints. His informed eye has largely shaped our perceptions of Canada's western mountains.

Landscape photography was central to his development as a mountain photographer. When Carole Harmon was about to begin the restoration of her grandfather's negatives, one photo archivist told her it would be wiser for her to make new photographs rather than undertake the tedious task of cleaning the old stock, making copy negatives, and identifying and cataloguing the collection. Ignorant of the works, he likely thought a mountain photographer took photos of mountains, a skill easy to acquire. In 'Mount Geikie and the Ramparts' (Plate 83), we see what seems an easy photograph to duplicate, except for its simplicity. The softness of foreground which we perceive first seduces us for the encounter with the formidable strength of the mountain beyond, the harsh but elegant stridency of the rock, the glacial coldness on the chiselled walls. Here the contrasts and paradoxes of mountain experience are idealized: timeless, yet shaped by time; inviting and repelling, giving life and taking it away relentlessly. The photograph crystallizes the rich and rare experience of the brief alpine summer and sums up our anticipations of the Rockies.

In Harmon's unpeopled landscapes we feel the rarely expressible awe that fills us when we are alone and silent on the margins of ice and rock. We see the mountains with his patterns of detailed foreground, a middle ground of slightly less interest, and a background of monumental stature. Among those who have made photographs in these mountain wildernesses, no other has had the patience and ambition or has created for himself so many opportunities to capture the mountains' diversity of mood, light, and season. The perception of landscape underlies Harmon's dramatization of the confrontations of man and nature. His achievement was to array the elements of the picturesque, as in 'Mount Geikie', then place people in the scene to humanize the setting while losing none of its glory, making his people larger than life because of their setting, and allowing them to enter the perpetual present of mythic time.

Rarest of Harmon's works are his salon photographs: images which tell no story, intimate no myth, are nearly void of a sense of place, and rely upon their abstract aesthetic appeal for their vigour. The bright zag of 'Waterfall' (Plate 82) is anonymous, striking, and apparently so elusive that many people

cannot tell what it is. They treat it as an expressionist work, turning it around in their hands trying to determine which way is up, hard pressed to make sense of it. It's similar to, if not as tickling as, the bizarre image of dog-team and skier (Plate 60), taken from a point of view we can describe only as cartographic.

Waterfalls haunt contemporary photographers. The essence of a waterfall is that it is continually in motion, a simple fact but one at odds with the idea of a photograph. Stopped too quickly, a waterfall is no longer a waterfall but a set of fixed droplets of water. Given too long an exposure, the contemporary cliché, the waterfall becomes an angel-hair semblance of a ziggurated Christmas tree, quite pretty, but deprived of its essence. In the Harmon work we are not robbed of the falling water's power or the swift dash and scatter on the glistening, blackened rocks, principally because the composition is so bold. The picture plane is almost severed, as though some giant had rent the earth asunder. The lightning brightness across the field of darkness, a metaphor of the photographic process in itself, rivets our attention before we know what the photograph captures. In 'Waterfall on the Castleguard River' (Plate 70) the lack of detail does not disturb us. The power and volume of the water, dwarfing the man standing before the fall, are what interests us. It is a photograph about scale, immensity, and nature, and it gains strength through its lack of detail.

'Lobby of the Banff Springs Hotel' (Plate 84) is a model

82 Waterfall. Lake of the Hanging Glaciers Expedition, 1920 or 1922.

of the importance of Byron Harmon's commercial photography. Probably taken under contract for the CPR or, less likely, for its postcard potential, the photograph is both an architectural and historical document. The hotel's major renovations before the Great War included the construction of the first part of the central tower and the new lobby, a splendid addition to the Canadian Rockies' premier hotel. When the baronial staircase dominating the lobby disappeared in further rebuilding in the 1920s, the lobby became more efficient, but most of its splendour was lost.

But the photograph is also a *tour de force* which demonstrates the skill and perceptions Harmon brought to a mundane task. Made in a period before artificial lighting was easily available, taken in a cavernously large room which is dim even today, the photograph is beautifully balanced in a warm, suffusing light. The long exposure through a nearly closed aperture gives the photograph super-realist qualities of detail and depth. We can inspect all the lobby's appointments: the ferns and spruces atop the rustic plant stands (themselves a whimsical decorative element which bespeaks the hotel's location at the nexus of sophistication and wildness, where the steamer-trunk set met the wilds and the natural world bowed to the unnatural), the spitoon beside the desk, the announcement board, the advertisement for Turkish baths, the patch of light punctuating the floor and giving the room a semblance of cathedral spaciousness.

83 Mount Geikie and the Ramparts, 1918.

84 Lobby of the Banff Springs Hotel, c. 1914.

In its accidental elements the picture comes to life. Accidents are infrequent in Byron Harmon's photographs, given his predilection for elaborate planning, the articulation of details, playing light and shadow in elegant *chiaroscuro*. In a hotel we like to believe is haunted, it is appropriate the lobby should have spectres, the ghosts of the long exposure. The three men near the pillar to the right are one; the two women behind the desk may be one; and the blur of the man reading the newspaper with the woman at the writing desk behind him is so chimerical we must believe it was built into the hotel. In the photograph we see a past the camera did not know was there.

In less obvious ways other photographs by Byron Harmon capture a fanciful past. The tales he was telling were well on their way to myth. The mountain West was a refuge for people who refused to move too rapidly into the twentieth century. In selecting the works for the present volume, we wanted to demonstrate Byron Harmon's facility with diverse subjects, concentrate on his principal themes and reveal his special interests: his love of faces, an aspect of characterization rather than a carryover from his earlier work in portraiture; his passion for the country above tree line, a black-and-white world so perfectly suited in its contrasts to his medium; and his fascination with the sensuousness of snow and glacial ice, to which he was drawn so compulsively we might suspect a 'Snow Queen' fable had some personal significance.

In the full range of the more than six thousand glass plates, nitrate negatives, negative copies, and prints which the Harmon family has given to the Peter Whyte Foundation in Banff, the diversity is remarkable. They include portraiture (formal, informal, and environmental); obvious postcard material, like 'Elsie Brooks with a bear' (Plate 37) or 'Mount Rundle and Echo Creek' (Plate 29); record shots for documentation that transcend their rationale, like 'A.O. Wheeler and T.G. Longstaff' (Plate 55); unusual and grotesque shots, like the haunting images of men in the mouths of ice or glacier caves (Plates 52, 62); action material, like the photograph of the immense snow cube falling from the roof of Glacier House (Plate 32), which suggests some of Robert Cumming's photography. Rare, wonderful and inimitable works.

Harmon's sense of humour was never cynical and rarely melancholy. Its pleasant chuckles, wry comment, and occasional exuberant silliness spread from the humorous photographs to illuminate the rest of his work. That ballet of awkwardness and grace that is the self-portrait of Byron up to his calves in water filming the fisherman is typical. He may have put his people into awkward places for the sake of a photograph, but the places were no less awkward for him.

The fellow in Plate 85 mocks pompous nobility. When we showed the picture to another man for identification, he said: 'It can't be Scotty Wright. He was a valley man. There's no way you'd find a man like him perched up on the top of a mountain.' Perhaps. But a photograph can easily make a mountain out of a minor promontory. Looking at the next page, we may wonder if that was the joke Scotty was in on.

85